30-DAY Bass Workout

An Exercise Plan for Bassists

David Overthrow

Alfred, the leader in educational publishing, and the National Guitar Workshop, one of America's finest guitar schools, have joined forces to bring you the best, most progressive educational tools possible. We hope you will enjoy this book and encourage you to look for other fine products from Alfred and the National Guitar Workshop.

This book was acquired, edited and produced by Workshop Arts, Inc., the publishing arm of the National Guitar Workshop.
Nathaniel Gunod: acquisitions, editor
Michael Rodman: editor
Gary Tomassetti: music typesetter
Timothy Phelps: interior design

Cover photos: Ted Engelbart/Karen Miller (photographers, lower left)
Greg Hyatt (model, lower left)
Larry Lyttle (photographer, upper right)

Copyright © MMI Alfred Publishing Co., Inc.
All rights reserved. Printed in USA.
ISBN 0-7390-2342-X

Contents

ABOUT THE AUTHOR 4

INTRODUCTION 5

SECTION ONE—TERMS, GEOGRAPHY AND READING MUSIC 6

SECTION TWO—BASIC TECHNIQUE 8
   Posture 8
   The Left Hand 9
   The Right Hand 10

SECTION THREE—THE BASIC WARM-UPS 12
   Warm-Up Exercise #1 12
   Warm-Up Exercise #2 13
   Warm-Up Exercise #3 14
   Warm-Up Exercise #4 15

SECTION FOUR—THE WORKOUTS....16
Using the Workouts 16
Day One 17
- Bassercise #1: 17
- Bassrobic #1: 17
Day Two 18
- Bassercise #2 18
- Bassrobic #2 18
Day Three 19
- Bassercise #3 19
- Bassrobic #3 19
Day Four 20
- Bassercise #4 20
- Bassrobic #4 20
Day Five 21
- Bassercise #5 21
- Bassrobic #5 21
Day Six 22
- Bassercise #6 22
- Bassrobic #6 22
Day Seven 23
- Bassercise #7 23
- Bassrobic #7 24
Day Eight 25
- Bassercise #8 25
- Bassrobic #8 25
Day Nine 26
- Bassercise #9 26
- Bassrobic #9 26
Day Ten 27
- Bassercise #10 27
- Bassrobic #10 27
Day Eleven 27
- Bassercise #11 27
- Bassrobic #11 27
Day Twelve 28
- Bassercise #12 28
- Bassrobic #12 28
Day Thirteen 29
- Bassercise #13 29
- Bassrobic #13 30
Day Fourteen 31
- Bassercise #14 31
- Bassrobic #14 32
Day Fifteen 33
- Bassercise #15 33
- Bassrobic #15 34
Day Sixteen 35
- Bassercise #16 35
- Bassrobic #16 36
Day Seventeen 36
- Bassercise #17 36
- Bassrobic #17 36
Day Eighteen 37
- Bassercise #18 37
- Bassrobic #18 37
Day Nineteen 38
- Bassercise #19 38
- Bassrobic #19 38
Day Twenty 38
- Bassercise #20 38
- Bassrobic #20 38
Day Twenty-One 39
- Bassercise #21 39
- Bassrobic #21 39
Day Twenty-Two 40
- Bassercise #22 40
- Bassrobic #22 40
Day Twenty-Three 41
- Bassercise #23 41
- Bassrobic #23 41
Day Twenty-Four 41
- Bassercise #24 41
- Bassrobic #24 42
Day Twenty-Five 42
- Bassercise #25 42
- Bassrobic #25 43
Day Twenty-Six 43
- Bassercise #26 43
- Bassrobic #26 43
Day Twenty-Seven 44
- Bassercise #27 44
- Bassrobic #27 44
Day Twenty-Eight 45
- Bassercise #28 45
- Bassrobic #28 45
Day Twenty-Nine 46
- Bassercise #29 46
- Bassrobic #29 46
Day Thirty 47
- Bassercise #30 47
- Bassrobic #30 47

About the Author

David Overthrow has been a bass faculty member at the National Guitar Workshop since its inception in 1983. He has performed with Mike Stern, John Abercrombie, Frank Gambalie, Trey Anastasio, Larry Coryell and many other notable artists. In addition to being a regular performer in the New York City and Connecticut areas, his playing can be heard on several CDs in styles including jazz, funk, rock, blues and reggae.

In addition to recording and performing, David Overthrow teaches at his private studio and is the Director of Music and Head of Jazz studies at the Canterbury School in New Milford, Connecticut.

David Overthrow endorses R&B basses, DR Handmade Strings and SWR Bass Amplifiers.

ACKNOWLEDGEMENTS
I would like to thank: My wonderful mother, my brother Keith, Yvette, Dave Smolover and Nat Gunod from the National Guitar Workshop, builder Ron Blake and his partner Ed Roman at R&B basses (www.worldclassguitars.com) for building my wonderful basses. Also thanks to Dave from SWR and Malcom from DR.

Other instructional books by David Overthrow:
The Complete Electric Bass Method
- Beginning Electric Bass
- Intermediate Electric Bass
- Mastering Electric Bass

Introduction

Technique is just one aspect of good playing. Although having good technique doesn't automatically make you a good bass player, it allows you to better execute and play your musical ideas.

This book is designed to help improve your technique. Practicing the exercises provided here will lead to improved left- and right-hand technique, particularly in the areas of alternate picking, coordination, dexterity, stamina and reach, to name a few.

There are several ways you can use this book:

1) Play through and learn all of the warm-ups and then proceed to the 30-day workout.

2) Select specific exercises to improve a particular aspect of your technique.

3) Work through all of the Bassercises in the 30-day workout. These are directed at developing your left-hand technique.

4) Work through all of the Bassrobics in the 30-day workout. These are directed at developing your right-hand technique.

5) Just play the warm-ups.

6) Play a new workout, including a Bassercise and a Bassrobic, each day for 30 days, and continue on this 30-day regimen.

It is recommended that you begin working through the book by playing through the warm-ups for several days. Then, as you work through the rest of the book, play through all four of the warm-ups before playing through the exercise of the day.

This book is meant to be just one resource of many to help you become a better bass player. Use this book along with other books, such as *The Complete Electric Bass Method*, to improve both as a musician and bass player. Most importantly, learn as many tunes as you can—in as many different styles as you can—and get out and play. There is no substitute for jamming and performing with others.

Enjoy!

Section One: Terms, Geography and Reading Music

Before we proceed and move on to the warm-ups, we need to review a few terms and symbols that you will need to know in order to play the exercises in this book.

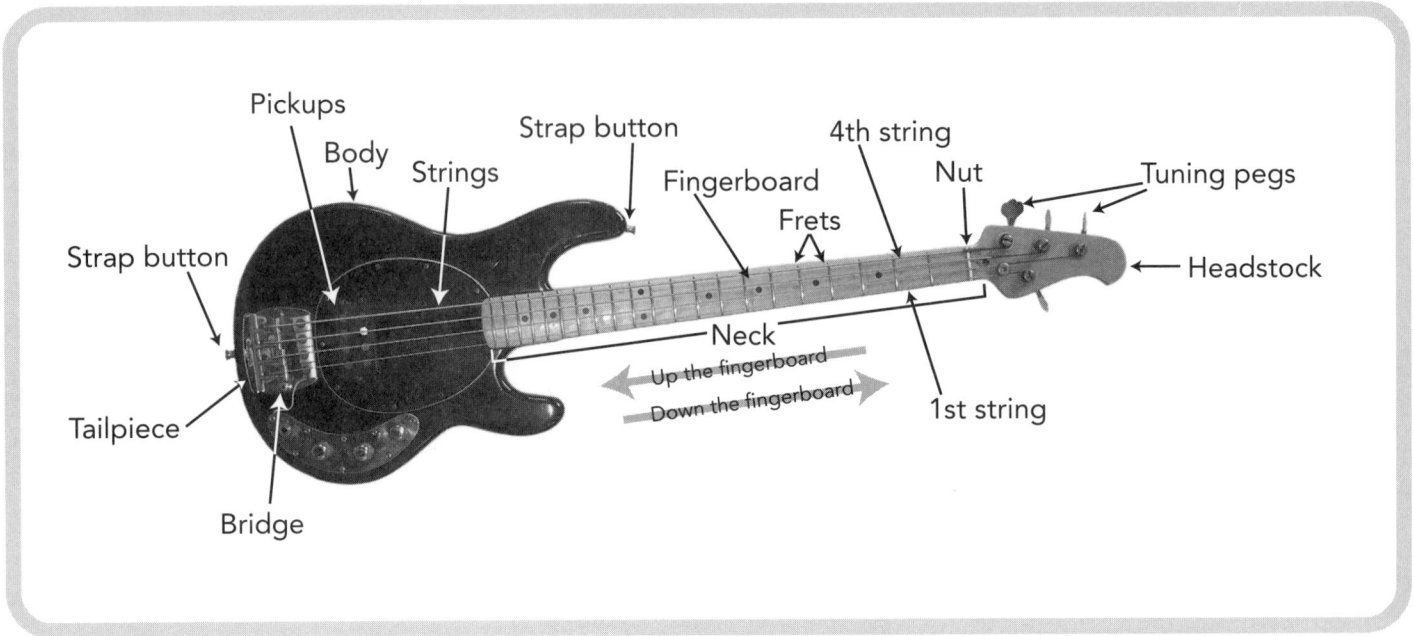

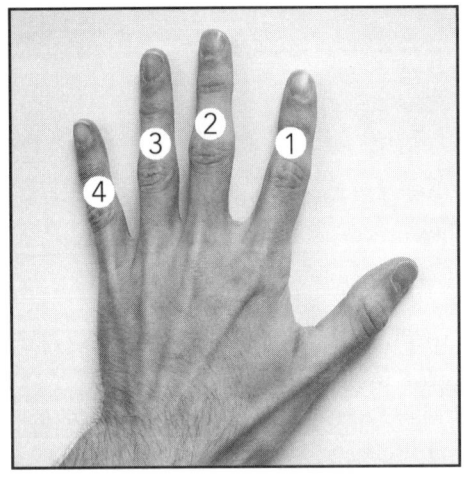

Left-hand finger numbers:

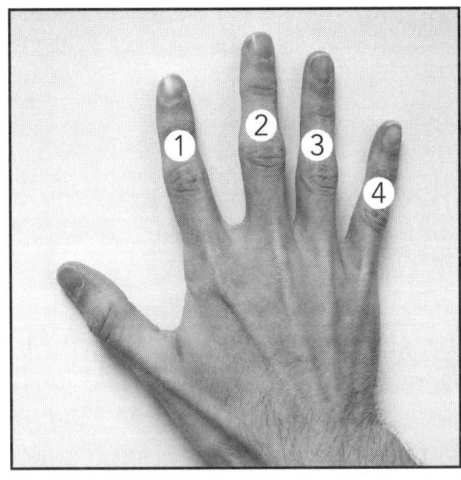

Right-hand finger numbers:

All of the examples in this book are shown in standard music notation and *tablature*.

Tablature

Tablature (TAB) is a system of notation that represents the strings of the bass. Each note is indicated by placing a number, which specifies the fret to play, on the appropriate string.

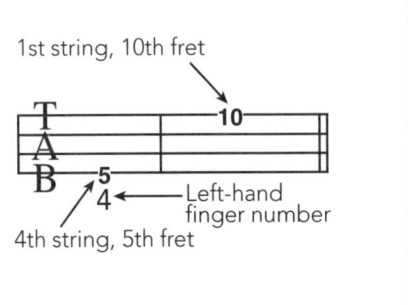

6 *SECTION ONE—Terms, Geography and Reading Music*

Standard Music Notation

Pitches on the Staff

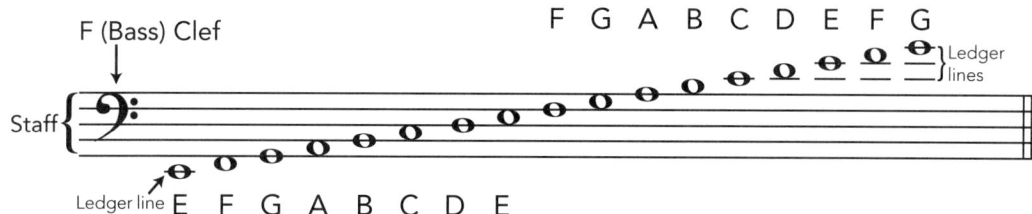

Accidentals

♯ = Sharp. Raise the note one fret (a *half step*).
♭ = Flat. Lower the note one fret (a half step).
♮ = Natural. Return the note to its normal position.

Measures and Bar Lines

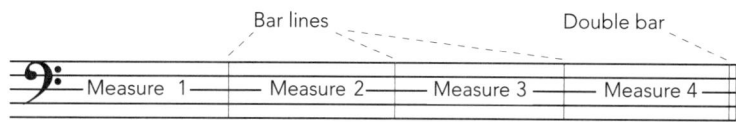

Note and Rest Values

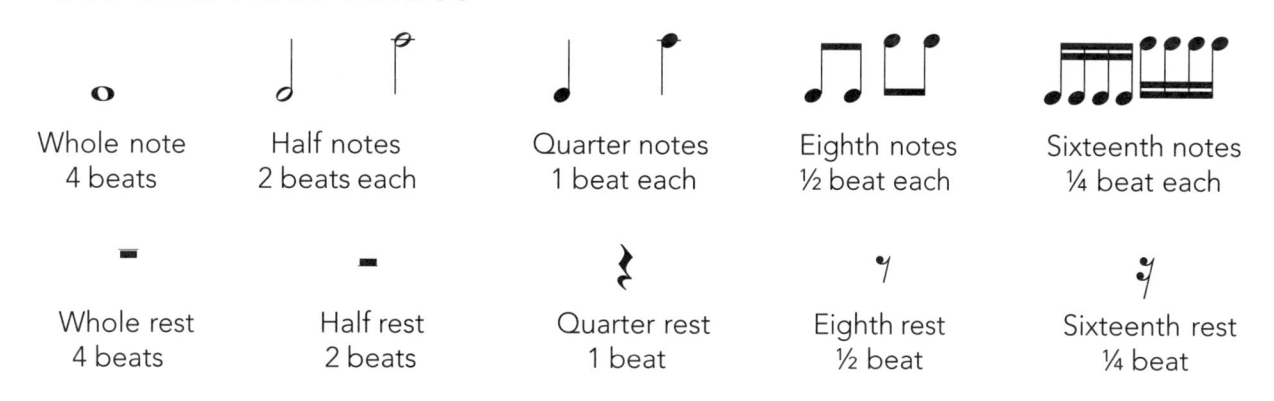

| Whole note | Half notes | Quarter notes | Eighth notes | Sixteenth notes |
| 4 beats | 2 beats each | 1 beat each | ½ beat each | ¼ beat each |

| Whole rest | Half rest | Quarter rest | Eighth rest | Sixteenth rest |
| 4 beats | 2 beats | 1 beat | ½ beat | ¼ beat |

Time Signatures

At the beginning of any piece of music you will find the *time signature*. A time signature consists of two numbers, one above the other. The top number tells us how many beats are in each measure. The bottom number tells us what kind of note gets one count.

4 ← 4 beats per measure
4 ← Quarter note ♩ = 1 beat

3 ← 3 beats per measure
4 ← Quarter note ♩ = 1 beat

The time signature you will come across most often is 4/4. For this reason, it is often called *common time* and is indicated by a 𝄴.

Section Two — Basic Technique

Posture

Posture is very important. Good posture will result in better endurance (being able to play longer), better focus and probably better playing overall. When playing sitting down, keep the following in mind:

- Your feet should be flat on the floor.
- Your back should be straight and upright.
- Breathe and focus.
- Your shoulders should be relaxed.

These points may seem obvious but they are very important. If you slouch or forget to breathe deeply, your brain cannot send messages as fast as it should and this *does* affect your playing!

Good posture

Using a Mirror
Practicing in front of a mirror can be very helpful. Looking in the mirror can help ensure that you are practicing with good posture. Also, if you are looking in the mirror, you are not staring at your hands. Bassists who stare at their hands as they practice are only *hearing* about 10% of what they are playing. If you practice without looking at your hands, it is more likely that you will hear 100% of what you are playing. If you do not use your eyes to control your hands, your ears will take over—and listening is the most important part of making great music!

Sitting and Standing
We must use a strap when standing to play the electric bass. Try to distribute your weight evenly and avoid putting it all on one foot. When playing with a strap, the position of the bass relative to your body should be the same as when playing seated. Most good players do not wear their basses below their waist or around their knees.

If you have a bass that is balanced correctly, it will keep extra weight off of your left shoulder. Many basses are built a little "neck heavy." If this is true of your bass, adjust the strap to hold the bass at a height that is comfortable for you and doesn't put extra weight on your shoulder.

Sitting

Standing

If you play left-handed, you will need to reverse many of the instructions in this book.

The Left Hand
The Thumb

The left-hand thumb should be placed on the back of the neck, with the ball of the thumb in the center of the neck's curve. The thumb mirrors the movement of the 2nd finger moving along the neck. Someone standing in front of you as you play should not see your thumb at all, as it would be hidden behind the neck.

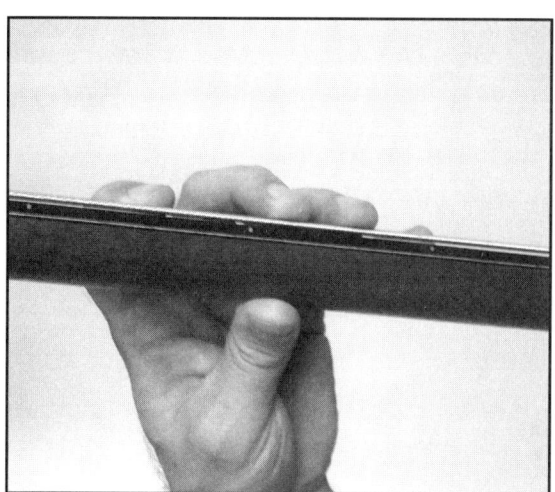

Thumb behind the neck, opposite the 2nd finger

Arching the Fingers

The fingers of the left hand should arch out in front of the fingerboard. Both joints of the fingers should bend to allow the fingertips to press the string to the fretboard. When pressing, use only as much pressure as you need to produce the note. Don't exert more pressure than necessary. Relaxation will help give you a good tone and lessen the chances of any muscular problems.

Left-hand fingers arch out in front of the fingerboard

Economy of Movement

The less distance you move your left hand, the better. When raising your fingers off the fingerboard, try to keep the finger just above the string, rather than an inch or two above it. Minimizing the size of your movements will allow you to play faster and more smoothly.

SECTION TWO—Basic Technique

The Right Hand

The right-hand fingers should not be held straight and should not be strained or tightened, but should be relaxed as you prepare to pluck the string. The tighter your muscles are held, the harder your attack on the string. If your hand is relaxed, it will help produce a softer attack and a better, more full-sounding tone.

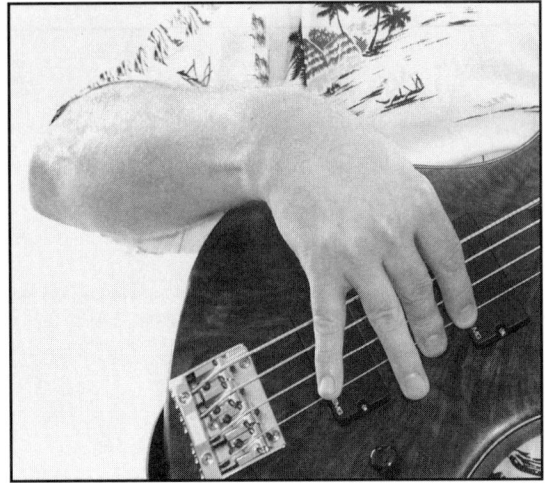
Tight right hand

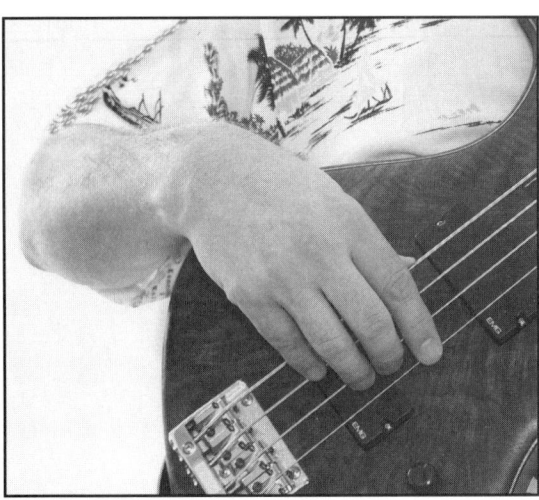
Relaxed right hand

Anchoring the Thumb

The thumb of the right hand should be anchored on your bass. Many players rest it on one of the pickups or even the lowest string, depending on which strings they are playing and what kind of tone they are striving for. If you rest your thumb on the bridge pickup, the result will be a bright tone. If you anchor your thumb on the neck pickup, you will achieve a darker, warmer tone. When playing the 1st or 2nd strings, you may find the lowest string is a good resting place for your thumb.

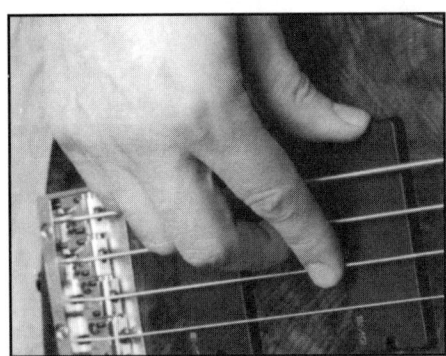
Thumb anchored on the pickup

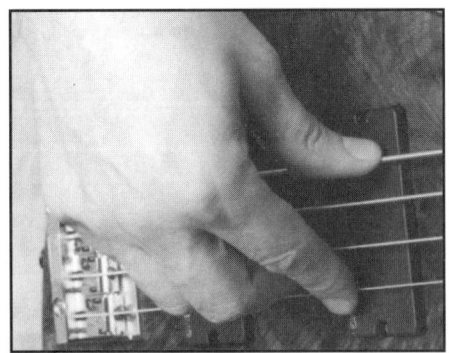
Thumb rested on the lowest string when playing the upper strings

Finger Alternation

Most players use both the 1st and 2nd fingers of the right hand to pluck the strings. When alternating your 1st and 2nd fingers, strive for an even sound. At first, your 2nd finger may be a little weaker, therefore the tone produced from this finger will not be as strong. The more you practice alternating your fingers as you play, the more even the sound will become. It is recommended that you use two fingers instead of one, as this will allow you to be a more versatile player.

REST STROKE

In *rest stroke*, the finger rests on the adjacent (next lower) string after it plucks. Here's how to do the rest stroke on the 1st string:

- Rest your 1st finger on the 1st string
- Slowly put pressure on the finger until it passes across the string
- Follow through with the finger until it is resting on the 2nd string

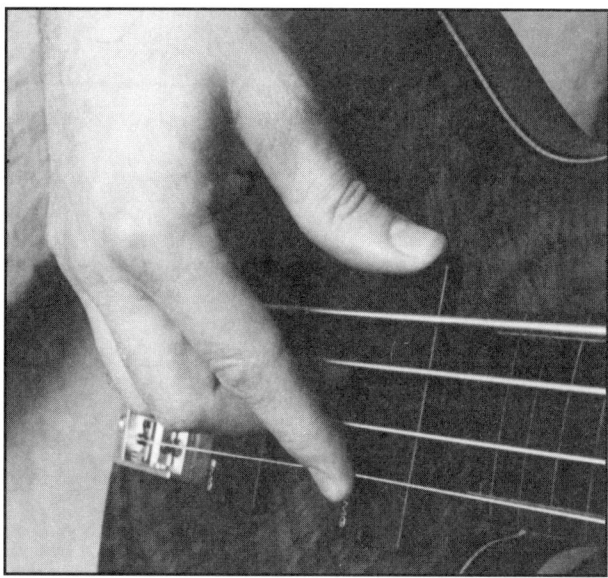

Before plucking

After plucking

Section Three — The Basic Warm-Ups

If you have ever tried to jog or play any sport without first warming up or stretching, you probably discovered that you couldn't perform up to your potential. This is often the cause of sports injuries. Playing the bass guitar also involves quite a bit of physical strength and the use of many different muscles in the hands. When bass players such as Victor Wooten and Stanley Clarke have a gig, they do not simply pick up the bass and play their hardest lightning-fast licks without warming up. The warm-up gradually stretches the muscles in the hands and prepares them for licks and bass lines that require dexterity, strength and agility.

The following warm-up routine consists of four exercises, two for the right hand and two for the left. Even if you don't have time for an entire practice session, these warm-ups are perfect to play through just before a gig and will help get your hands loose enough to play with a minimum level of tension.

Warm-Up Exercise #1
Stretch and Relax

This exercise should be played slowly and with ease. Remember that we are not concerned with speed in this exercise but simply getting the muscles in the hand to stretch and relax. The more relaxed the hand, the better off you are. When pressing the string to the fingerboard, use just enough pressure to produce the note. Don't use more energy than necessary. Pressing with maximum force may lead to muscle cramps or other problems in your left hand and forearm. And besides, playing in a relaxed manner will help you develop a great sound.

If you have a metronome, set it to a slow *tempo* (speed), such as ♩ = 60, for these exercises. If you don't, just count slowly.

Let's play the exercise. The process is illustrated with fret diagrams at the top of the next page. First play F at the 1st fret of the 4th (lowest) string and hold it for four beats. As your 1st finger continues to hold the F, place the 2nd finger on the F♯ at the 2nd fret of the 4th string and slowly count to four again. Keeping pressure on the first two fingers, place the 3rd finger at the 3rd fret and play the G while counting to four. Finally play the G♯ at the 4th fret with your 4th finger. At this point all fingers should be pressing the 4th string to the fingerboard.

Now, release all notes from the fingerboard and play the F at the 1st fret once again. Place the 2nd finger at the 2nd fret and play the F♯ as you did before. Play the G at the 3rd fret with the 3rd finger. Then, play C♯ at the 4th fret of the *3rd string* with the 4th finger. At this point, pressure should be exerted on all four fingers. Next, play the first two notes on the 4th string and use the 3rd and 4th fingers on the 3rd string. Then play the 1st fret on the 4th string and the 2nd, 3rd and 4th frets of the 3rd string. Finally, play the first four frets on the 3rd string, counting four beats for each note. Repeat this process starting on the 3rd and 2nd strings.

Warm-Up Exercise #1

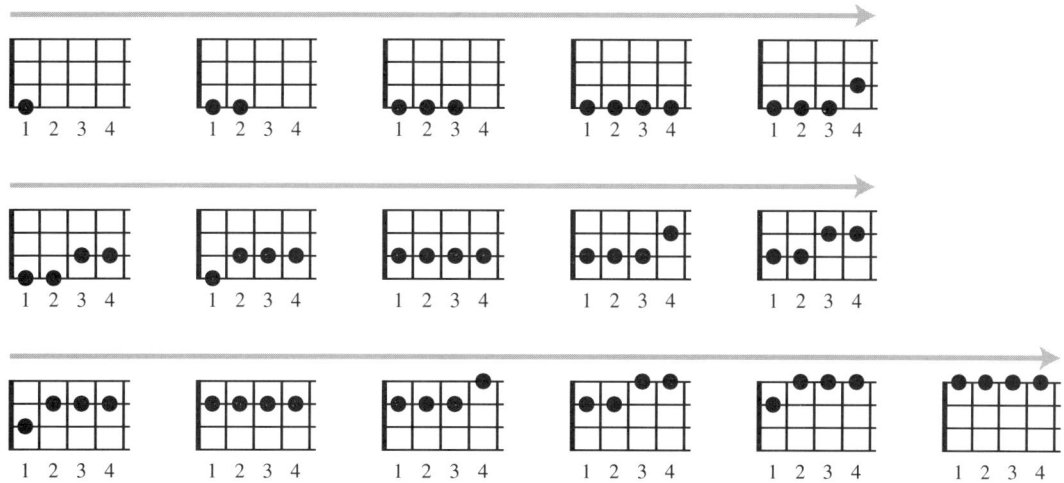

Warm-Up Exercise #2
Pizzicato/Alternating Fingers

Although some bass players use just the 1st finger of their right hand to pluck the strings, most players use two fingers to play and in some instances, three. The challenge when using two or more fingers is to get an even sound—the fingers should sound alike. Always strive to get an even sound. This will help your playing sound smooth.

When playing open strings, it is important to stop the string from sounding when you are done with the note. For example, when you are finished playing the eighth notes on the open 1st string in the first measure of Exercise #2 (below), you should stop the 1st string from sounding before playing the open 2nd string in the next measure. To do this, simply use two or more fingers of your left hand to damp the string and stop it from sounding.

Make sure you use two or more fingers to damp. If you damp the string with only one finger and place it over a fret, a harmonic may sound.

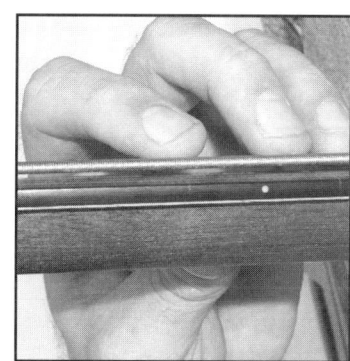

Use two or more fingers of your left hand to damp the open string.

Remember to consistently alternate your 1st and 2nd fingers while plucking the strings.

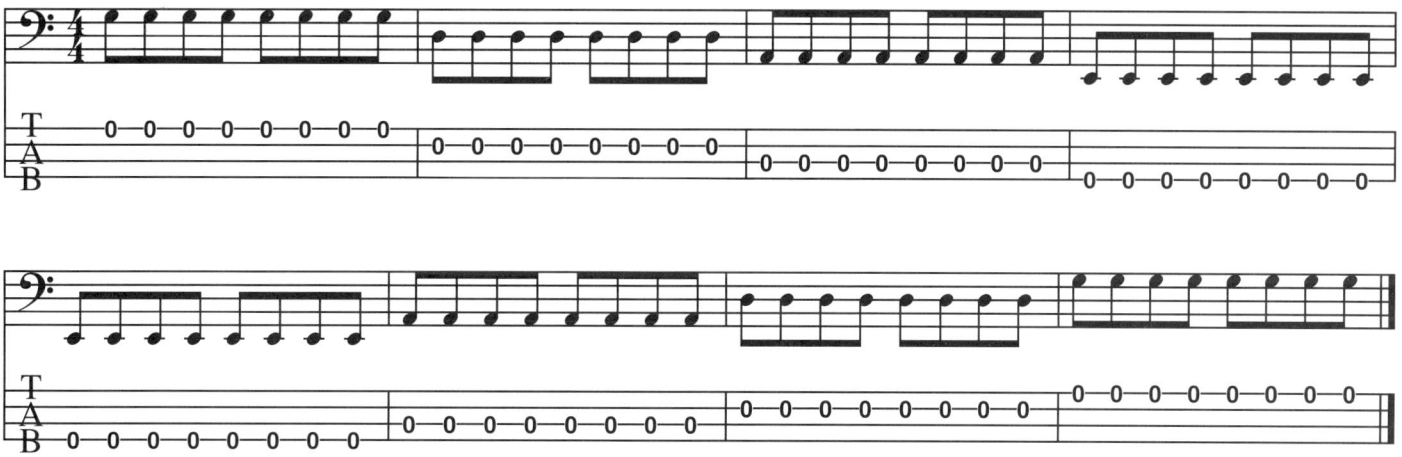

Warm-Up Exercise #3
Fingers of Freedom

A

The following exercise will get your left-hand muscles stretched and prepare them to play bass lines that require dexterity and agility. First, play the B♭ at the 1st fret of the 3rd string. Play the F on the 2nd string, keeping the 1st finger down on the B♭. You will probably feel the muscles stretching. Now, as you hold down the B♭ and F, play the high B♭ at 3rd fret of the 1st string with the 4th finger. All three fingers should now be pressed to the fingerboard. You will definitely feel the muscles stretching. Remember not to press with maximum force. Use just enough pressure to press the strings to the fingerboard.

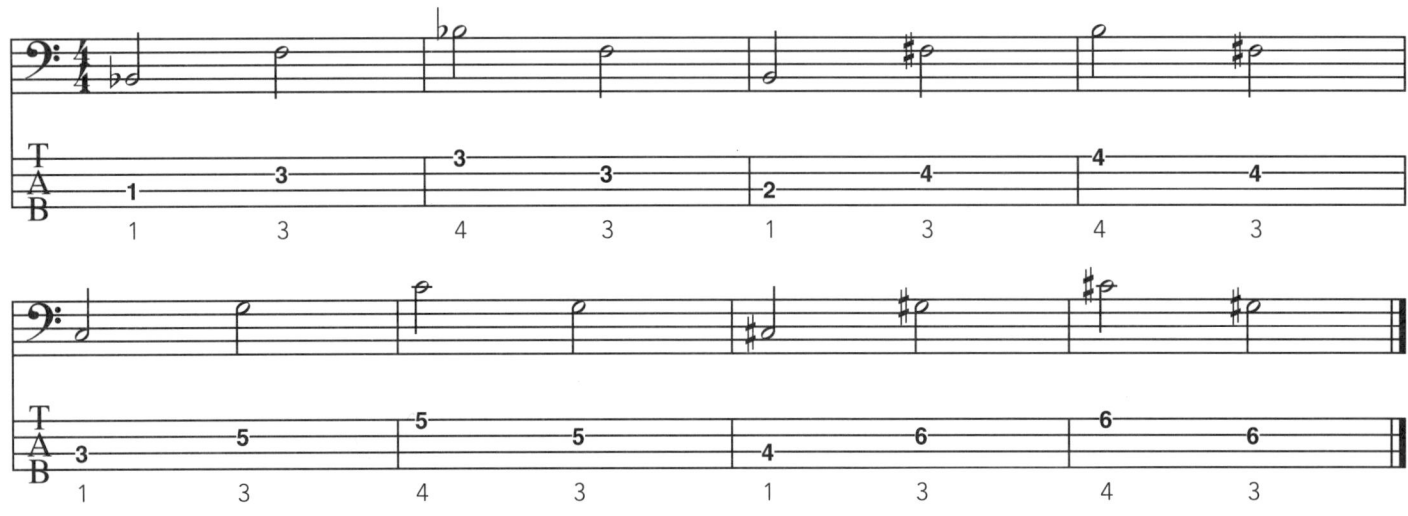

B

This is a similar exercise as #3A but is played on the 2nd, 3rd and 4th strings. Have fun!

14 *SECTION THREE—The Basic Warm-Up*

Warm-Up Exercise #4
Good for Both Hands

A
This exercise is a warm-up for both the right and left hands. When playing this exercise, make sure to alternate the fingers of your right hand. Play slowly at first. Roll your left-hand fingers from the 4th string to the 3rd string by collapsing the joint at the tip of the finger.

B
This is the same exercise, played on the 2nd and 3rd strings.

C
This is the same exercise, played on the 1st and 2nd strings.

SECTION THREE—The Basic Warm-Up

Section Four — The Workouts

The rest of the book contains 30 separate workouts called "Bassercises" and "Bassrobics." These exercises are designed to help you gain a level of technical proficiency on the bass by improving your dexterity and agility. The workouts will help you play bass lines that demand a high degree of technical facility by building strength and coordination in both the right and left hands. Each day of the workout begins with the four warm-up exercises you learned in Section Three. Always keep in mind the importance of good posture and correct hand position. Otherwise, you may develop bad habits and not enjoy the optimum benefits of doing the exercises.

Using the Workouts

Each day has at least one Bassercise and one Bassrobics excercise. Some have more. You can use the book two different ways. The first method is recommended if you are at the beginning to early intermediate levels of playing; the second method is for late-intermediate to advanced players.

1) Divide the book into two 30-day workouts. For the first 30 days, play only the Bassercises, following the order of the book. They will help you build strength in your left hand.

   After you have finished the Bassercises, spend 30 days playing through all of the Bassrobics exercises in order (don't forget to do the warm-ups, first!). This will help you build strength and dexterity in your right hand. After you finish the Bassrobics, you can continue to alternate between the two 30-day workouts until you have enough strength and stamina to play both exercises each day.

2) Each day, play both the Bassercise and one Bassrobics exercises.

Regardless of which method you choose, these exercises will help strengthen both your hands. Even if you are not presently playing gigs, they will prepare you for the day when that one phone call could get your bass-playing career started.

> NOTE:
> Many exercises include instructions to play them **"chromatically up and down the fingerboard and across all four strings."** This means to:
>
> - Play the same finger pattern, without alteration of any kind, but starting on the next higher fret (chromatically means "movement by half step," which is one fret). Repeat the pattern again and again, one fret higher each time, until you have run out of fingerboard. Then, play the exact same pattern, starting one fret lower. Continue to repeat the pattern, one fret lower each time, until you reach the starting point.
>
> - Pause and rest.
>
> - Do all of that again, but on another string. Do this until you have played the exercise on all four strings.

Take a deep breath and let's begin our first day of workouts.

Day One

Warm-Ups #1–4
Bassercise #1

Play this exercise slowly. Concentrate on getting a good sound on each note. Make sure to use just the tips of your left-hand fingers and alternate the right-hand fingers.

Bassrobic #1

This exercise is similar to Bassercise #1, but the rhythm played by the right hand is twice as fast. Concentrate on making an even tone with the 1st and 2nd fingers of the right hand. Use the fingertips of the left hand.

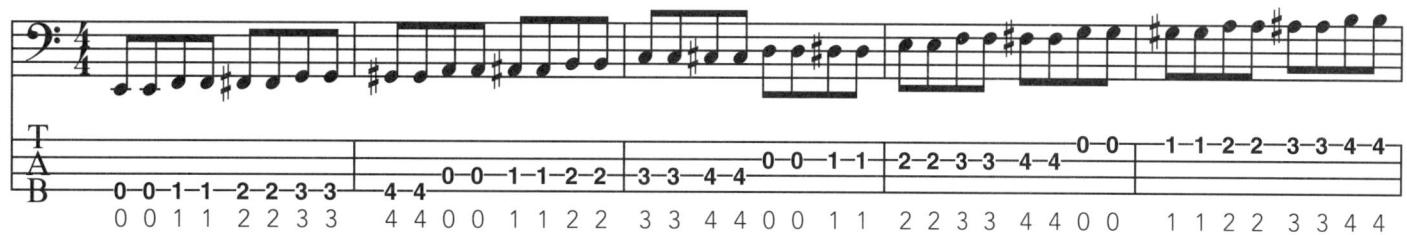

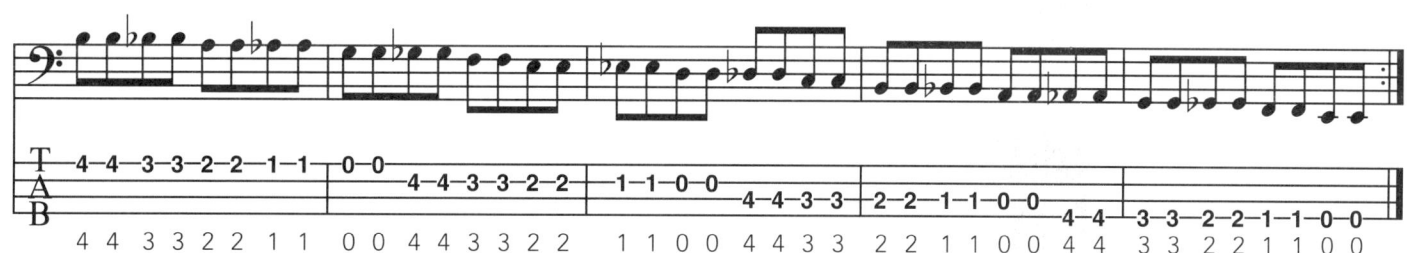

Day Two

Warm-Ups #1–4
Bassercise #2

This is a chromatic exercise using eight-note groups. After playing the first group of eight notes, move a half step up the fingerboard and play another eight-note group just like it. This is called a *sequence*. Repeat this process until you run out of fingerboard.

Then play the exercise descending. Here is an example of how to practice the same pattern descending, from a higher position down.

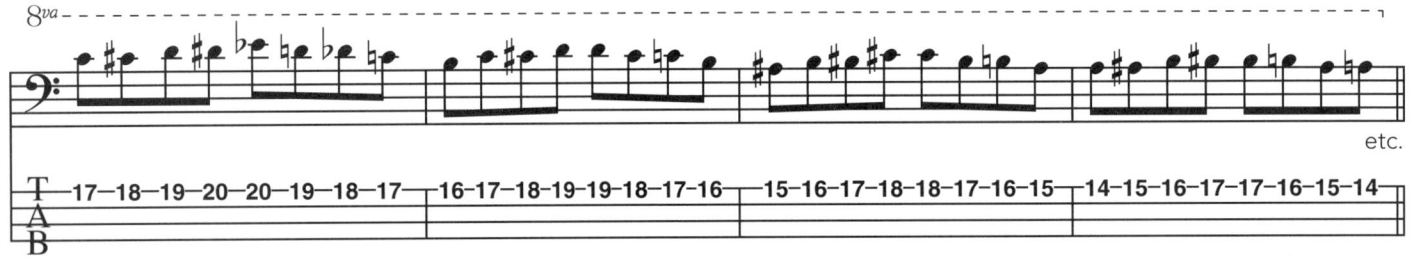

8va = Play an octave (twelve half steps) higher than written.

This is a similar exercise. The only difference is that we move from string to string, across the different strings, instead of up or down the fingerboard.

Bassrobic #2

When playing this exercise, remember to alternate the fingers of your right hand. As your fingers ascend through the rising chromatic line in the first two beats of each measure, keep each finger down as you place the next.

18 SECTION FOUR—The Workouts

Day Three

Warm-Ups #1–4
Bassercise #3

Sequence the one-measure figure in this exercise up and down the fingerboard chromatically on each string. Play with an even tone and make sure your hands are relaxed.

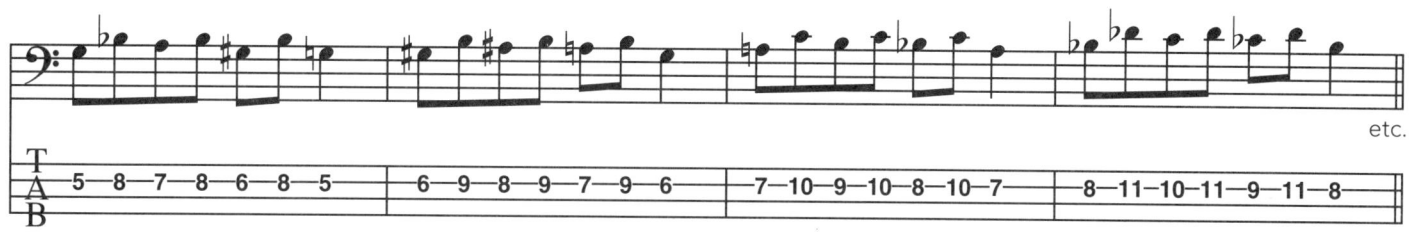

Bassrobic #3

This is also an exercise to be played up and down the fingerboard chromatically and across all four strings. As you play the sixteenth notes, be sure to alternate the fingers of the right hand. Concentrate on getting the same tone out of each finger.

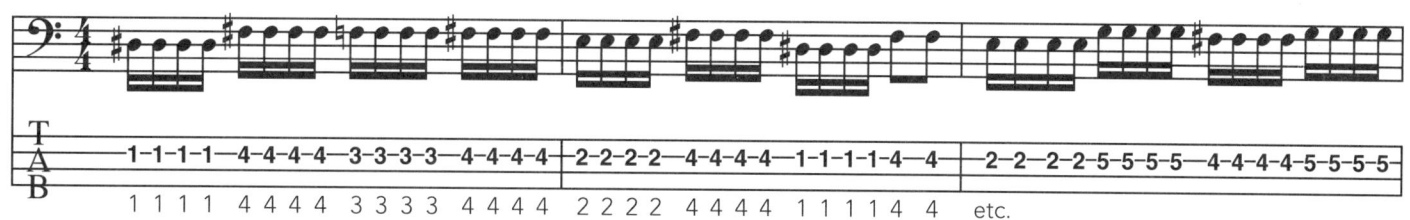

Day Four
Warm-Ups #1–4
Bassercise #4

Practice this pattern chromatically up and down the fingerboard. Concentrate on getting a good sound out of each note. Start by playing the exercise slowly and then gradually increase the tempo on each repetition. Also practice this pattern across the strings.

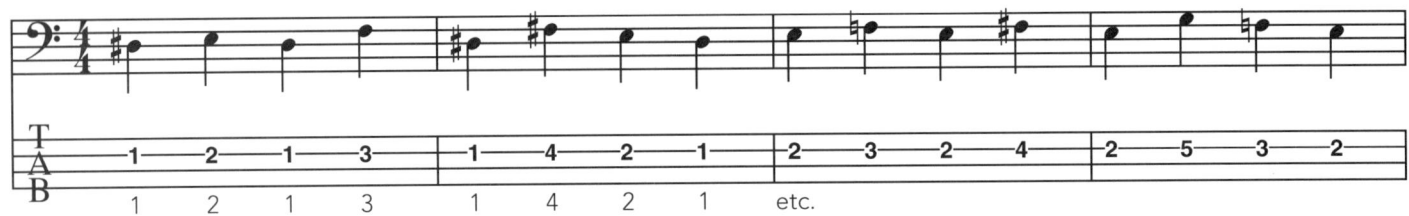

Bassrobic #4

This exercise involves playing eighth-note *triplets* (three notes in the time of two). Be sure to strive for an even tone. Alternate the 1st and 2nd fingers of your right hand, and notice how they alternate playing the first note of each triplet (**1st**-2nd-1st, **2nd**-1st-2nd, **1st**-2nd-1st, etc.). Make sure to play the exercise slowly at first, then gradually increase the tempo on each repetition.

Day Five

Warm-Ups #1–4
Bassercise #5

This exercise is a good workout for stretching from the 1st to the 2nd finger, and the 1st to the 3rd finger. It is in 6/4 time (six beats per measure). Play this exercise chromatically up and down the fingerboard and across all four strings.

Bassrobic #5

Play this pattern chromatically up and down the fingerboard. Concentrate on getting a good sound out of each note. Also practice this pattern across all strings. Start by playing the exercise slowly, and gradually accelerate to faster tempos on each repetition. While alternating your 1st and 2nd fingers, strive for evenness of both tone and rhythm.

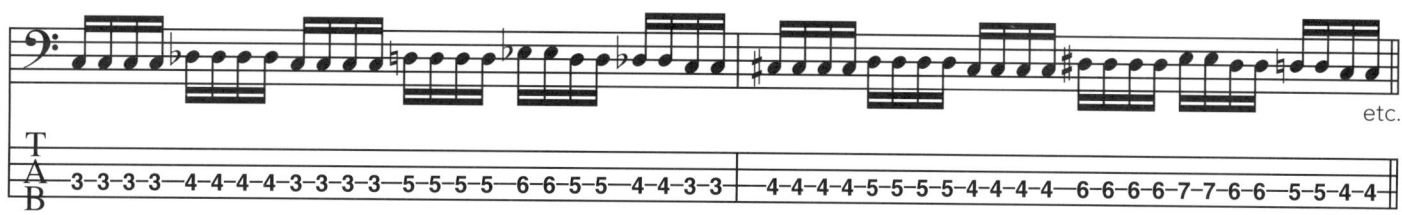

Day Six
Warm-Ups #1–4
Bassercise #6

Play this pattern chromatically up and down the fingerboard. Also practice this pattern across all four strings. Start by playing the exercise slowly and then gradually accelerate to faster tempos.

Bassrobic #6

Play this pattern chromatically up and down the fingerboard and across all four strings. Concentrate on getting a good sound out of each note. Start by playing the exercise slowly and then gradually increase the tempo. Keep the sound of the alternating right-hand fingers even.

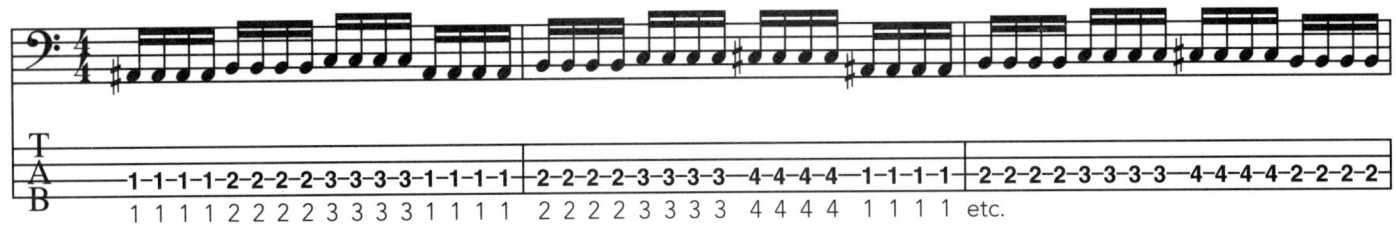

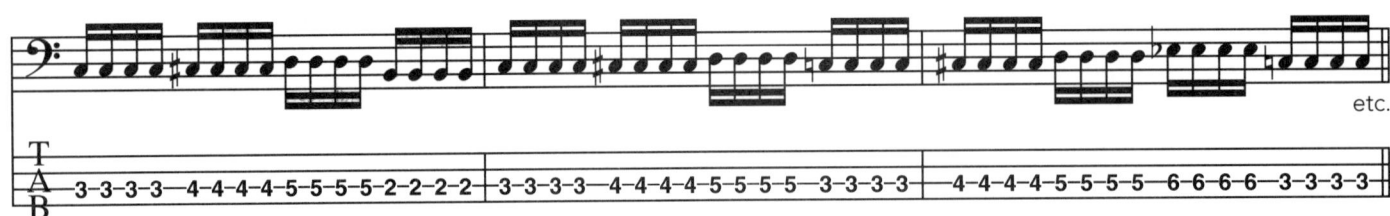

Day Seven
Warm-Ups #1–4
Bassercise #7

As you may have noticed, we have been exploring different left-hand fingering combinations. Playing these exercises is not a substitute for practicing scales and chords or learning tunes. It should be a *part* of your practice regimen. These workouts are helping you master the physical aspect of playing the bass. Here's another one-measure pattern to sequence chromatically.

Jaco Pastorius hit the jazz scene in a major way in 1976. In that single year, he recorded with Pat Metheny, Weather Report and Al DiMeola, in addition to recording his own album. He influenced an entire generation of electric bass players.

SECTION FOUR—The Workouts

Bassrobic #7

Play this two-measure pattern chromatically up and down the fingerboard. Strive for good tone! Also practice this pattern across all four strings. Start by playing the exercise slowly and then increase to faster tempos.

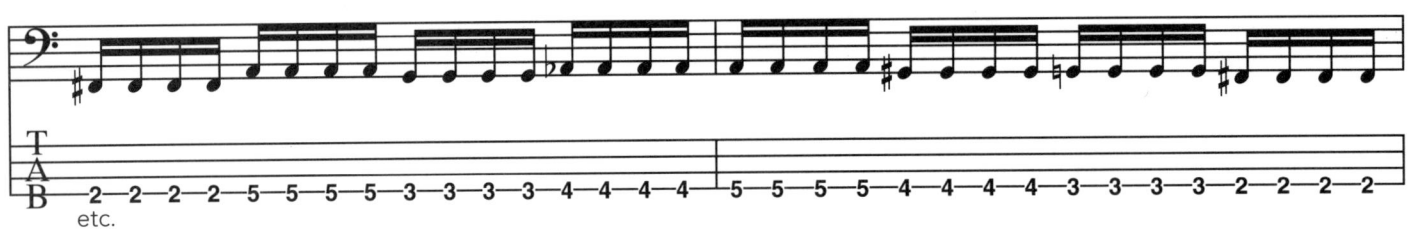

Day Eight
Warm-Ups #1–4
Bassercise #8

Notice that the time signature of this exercise is 3/4. Play this four-measure pattern chromatically up and down the fingerboard. Concentrate on getting a good sound out of each note. Also practice this pattern across all four strings. Start by playing the exercise slowly and then gradually increase the tempo.

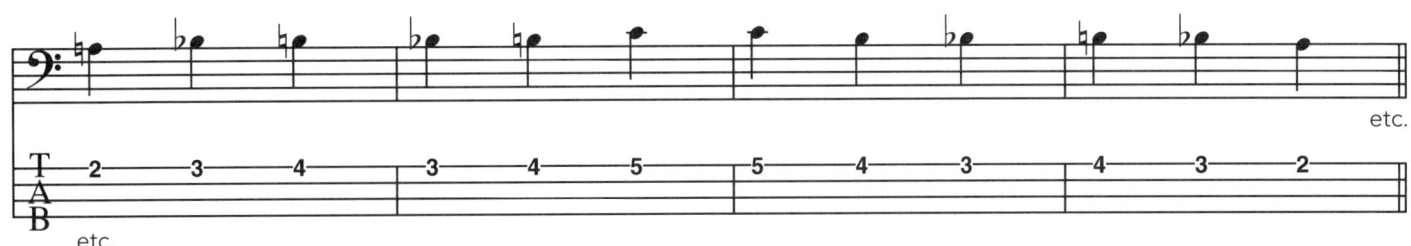

Bassrobic #8

This exercise involves playing triplets with the right hand. Play this four-measure pattern chromatically up and down the fingerboard. Work on your tone and practice across all four strings. Play slowly until it is mastered and then accelerate to faster tempos.

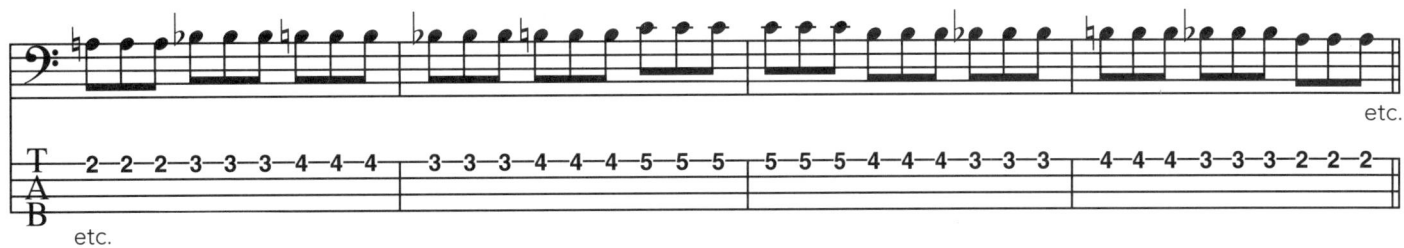

SECTION FOUR—The Workouts

Day Nine
Warm-Ups #1–4
Bassercise #9

Notice that the time signature of this exercise is 6/4. The last group of eighth notes in each measure covers a distance of five frets and is played with the 1st, 2nd and 4th fingers. This long stretch in your left hand is called an *extended fingering*. As with all of the exercises, Bassercise #9 should be sequenced chromatically up and down the fingerboard. Concentrate on getting a good sound out of each note. This pattern is written starting on the 2nd string but be sure to practice it across all four strings. Start slowly and then gradually speed up.

Bassrobic #9

This exercise involves playing triplets in the right hand. Notice the 1st and 2nd fingers alternate playing the first note of each triplet (**1st**-2nd-1st, **2nd**-1st-2nd, **1st**-2nd-1st, etc.). While alternating your 1st and 2nd fingers, strive for even-sounding triplets, in terms of both tone and rhythm. As with all of the exercises, Bassrobic #9 should be sequenced chromatically up and down the fingerboard.

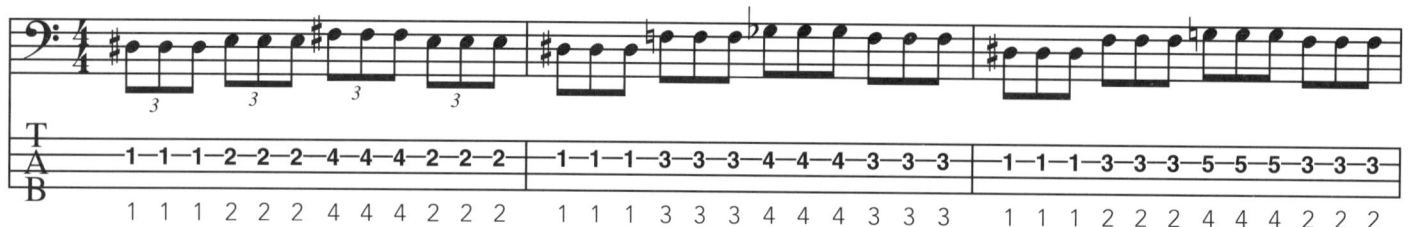

Day Ten
Warm-Ups #1–4
Bassercise #10
Bassrobic #10

Today is the first of your review days. Practice the exercises for Days 1–4. Make sure to practice each across all four strings of the bass. This might be a good time for you to try playing the exercises at even faster tempos.

If you are only playing Bassercises on this pass through the book, then just review those for Days 1–4. If you are only playing Bassrobics, then just review those for Days 1–4.

Day Eleven
Warm-Ups #1–4
Bassercise #11
Bassrobic #11

Today is the second of your review days. Practice the exercises for Days 5–9. Practice each one across all four strings of the bass. Try even faster tempos.

If you are only playing Bassercises on this pass through the book, then just review those for Days 5–9. If you are only playing Bassrobics, then just review those for Days 5–9.

Geddy Lee
Rush is one of the most innovative supergroups to come out of the mid-1970s. Geddy Lee's biting, complex bass lines are largely responsible for the band's unique sound.

SECTION FOUR—The Workouts

Day Twelve

Warm-Ups #1–4
Bassercise #12

These are three-note groupings using *tritone* intervals (six half steps). Patterns A and C are written starting on the 4th string, while patterns B and D are written starting on the 3rd string. Sequence each pattern chromatically up and down the fingerboard. Relax the left hand to allow the fingers to stretch easily.

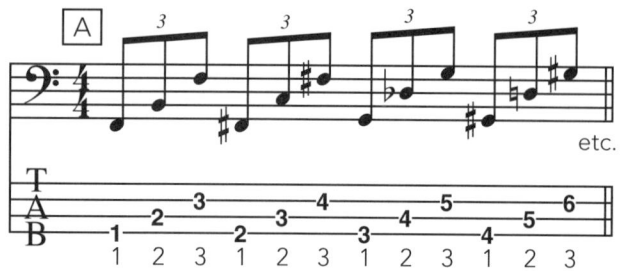

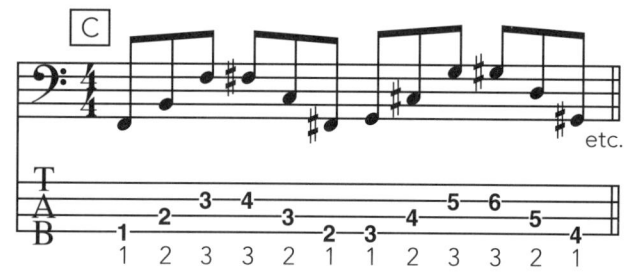

Bassrobic #12

This exercise gives your right hand a workout playing eighth-note triplets while playing tritone intervals with the left hand. Be sure to alternate the 1st and 2nd fingers of your right hand. Remember to keep your left hand relaxed to make the stretches easier. Also concentrate on maintaining a good, even tone.

This exercise is a tritone workout starting on the 3rd string. The stretch here is not as far as the one in the previous exercise, but you should continue to concentrate on keeping your left hand relaxed.

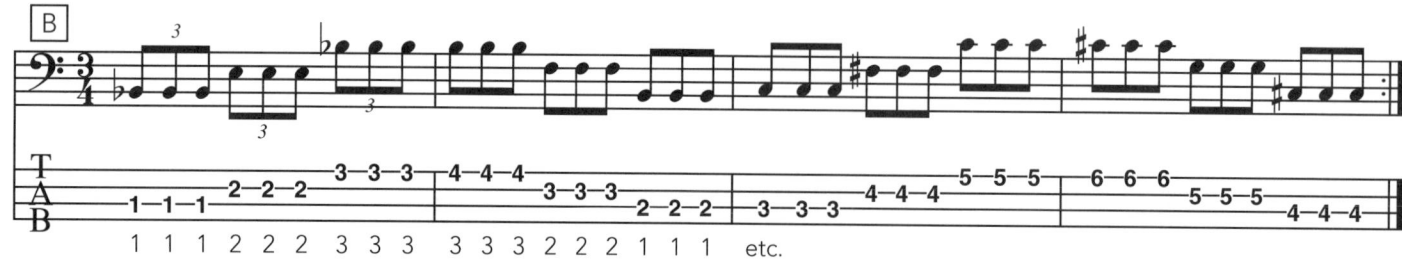

Day Thirteen

Warm-Ups #1–4
Bassercise #13

These exercises give your left hand a workout by including tritone intervals in four-note groupings. In the lowest positions the stretch is quite large, but it will get smaller as you ascend the fingerboard. Play all three of these exercises chromatically up and down the fingerboard. Play them slowly at first and then gradually increase the tempo.

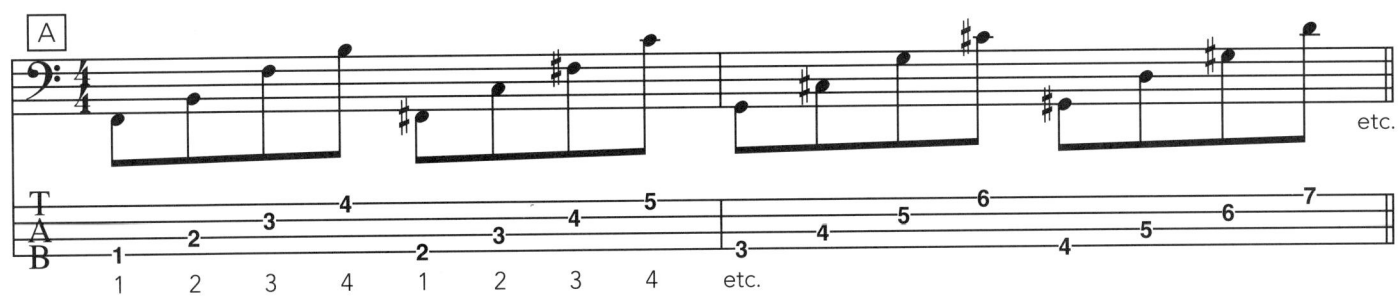

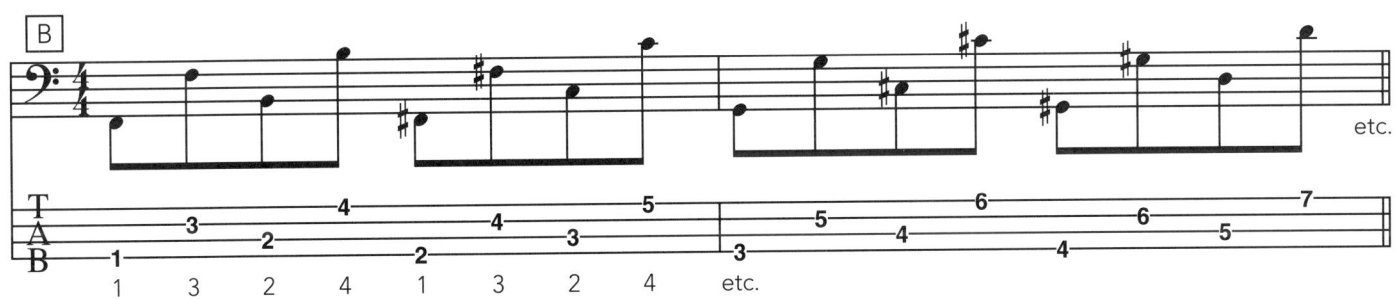

SECTION FOUR—The Workouts

Bassrobic #13

These exercises continue to explore the tritone interval. While the left hand gets a stretch workout playing the intervals, the right hand gets a workout playing eighth-note triplets. Sequence all three of these exercises chromatically up and down the fingerboard. As always, start slowly and then gradually increase the tempo.

Day Fourteen
Warm-Ups #1–4
Bassercise #14

These exercises are based on dominant 7* *arpeggios* (broken chords). Exercise A uses an extended fingering to play the arpeggio. This fingering requires a long stretch between the 1st and 4th fingers of the left hand. The fingering in exercise B allows you to play the arpeggio in one position. This fingering does not require as much of a stretch but you may feel the hand tighten as you sequence the pattern up and down the fingerboard. Concentrate on keeping both hands relaxed and making a good sound on each note.

The chord names of the arpeggios are shown above the music. Knowing what dominant chords you are playing will make this exercise more meaningful for you.

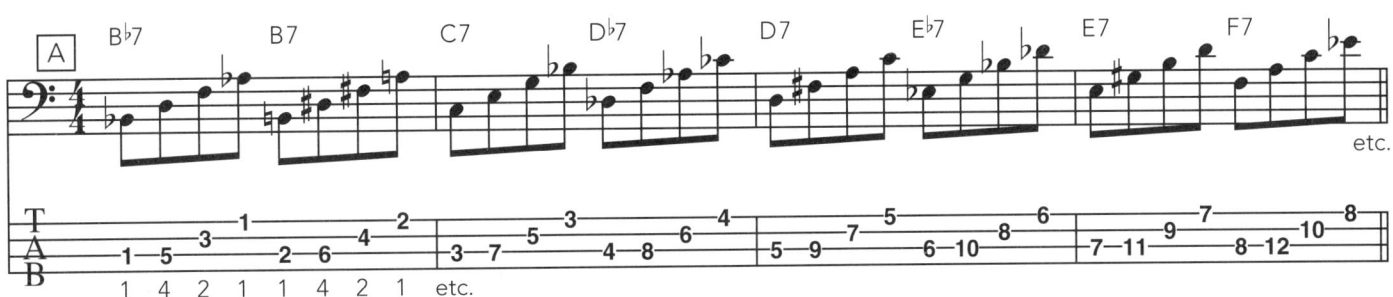

* The notes of a dominant 7 chord are root, 3, 5 and ♭7, refering to the notes that belong in the chord and their positions in a major scale that is built on the first note (root) of that chord. If you are unfamiliar with this concept, pick up my book *Beginning Electric Bass*, also from the National Guitar Workshop and Alfred. This music theory information is explained in detail in that book.

Bassrobic #14

This exercise will give your right hand a great workout. While your left hand plays dominant 7 arpeggios, your right hand plays rapid sixteenth notes. Practice starting on the 4th and 3rd strings and sequence the one-measure pattern chromatically up and down the fingerboard. Concentrate on maintaining an even tone with the alternating 1st and 2nd fingers of your right hand. Play slowly and relaxed, and gradually increase the tempo as you practice this exercise.

This is another exercise using dominant 7 arpeggios. Constantly alternate your right-hand fingers as you play the triplets. Practice starting on the 4th and 3rd strings and sequence the one-measure pattern chromatically up and down the fingerboard.

Day Fifteen
Warm-Ups #1-4
Bassercise #15

This exercise will give your left hand a fantastic workout by arpeggiating various chords (major 7, dominant 7, minor 7 and minor 7♭5 also called *half-diminished*). The fingering given is an extended fingering and requires a long stretch with the left hand. Make sure you play relaxed and slowly at first. Play starting on the 4th and 3rd strings and sequence the one-measure pattern chromatically up and down the fingerboard. Your hand may burn a bit after this one!

This exercise takes you through arpeggios like the one above does, but uses different fingerings. Play this exercise starting on the 4th and 3rds strings and sequence the series of arpeggios chromatically up and down the fingerboard.

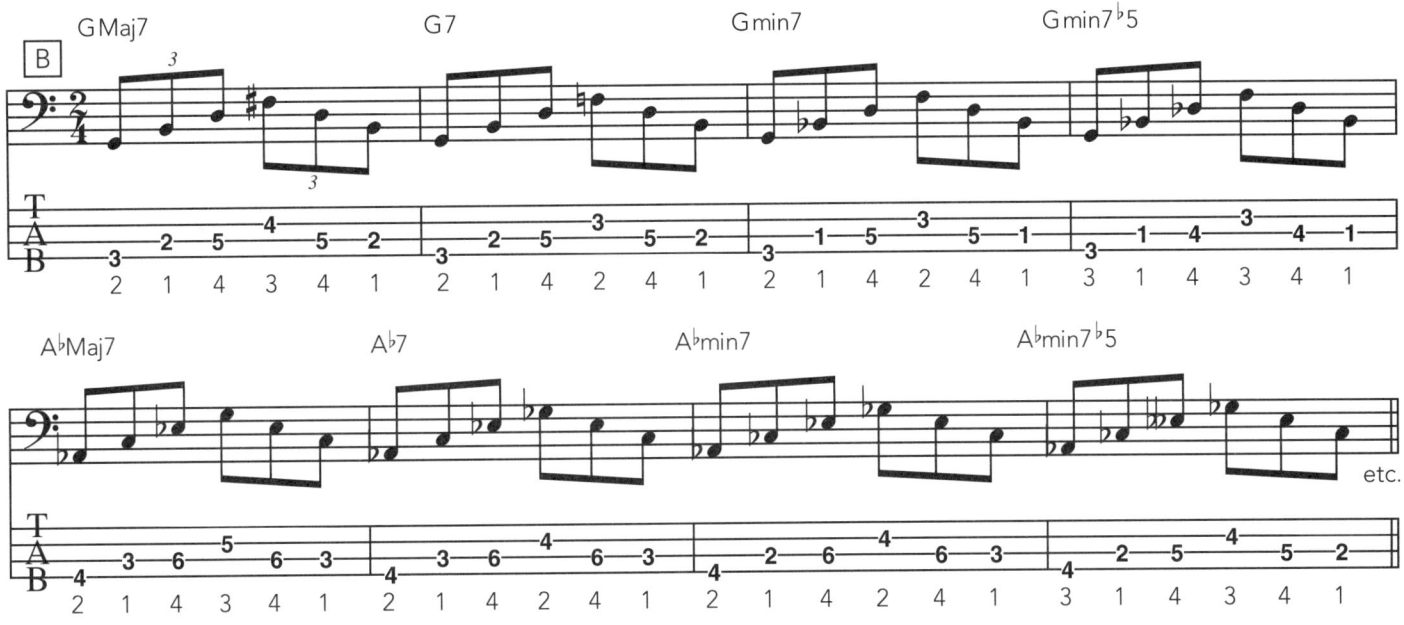

SECTION FOUR—The Workouts

Bassrobic #15

This exercise will give you a great workout, since it requires you to play 7 arpeggios in sixteenth-note triplets. Keep both hands very relaxed. Remember to alternate the 1st and 2nd fingers of the right hand and strive for an even sound. Practice starting on the 4th and 3rd strings and sequence the four-measure series of chords chromatically up and down the fingerboard. The series of chords is the same as yesterday's: Maj7, dominant 7, min7 and min7♭5. Take a deep breath, as you will need lots of stamina for this one!

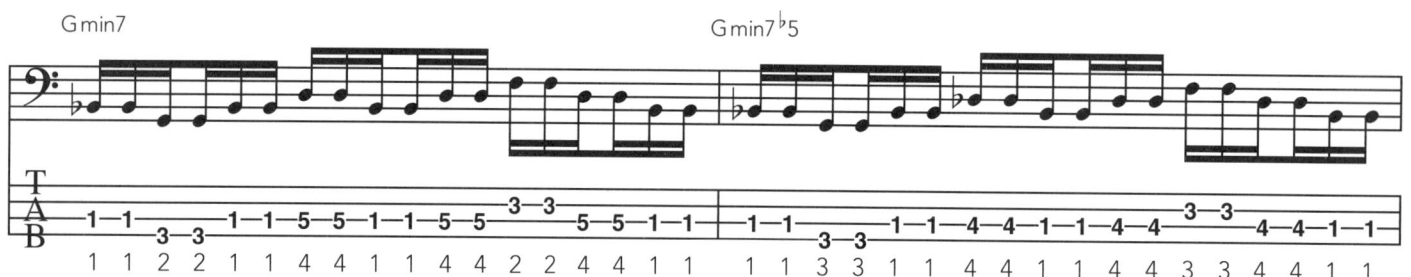

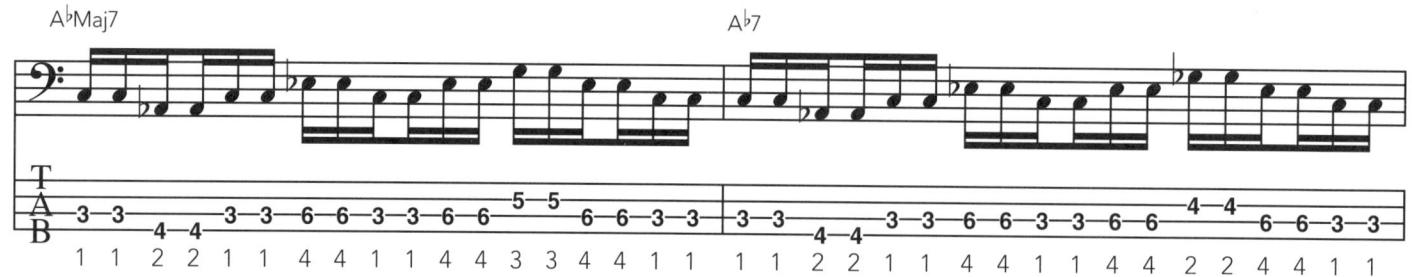

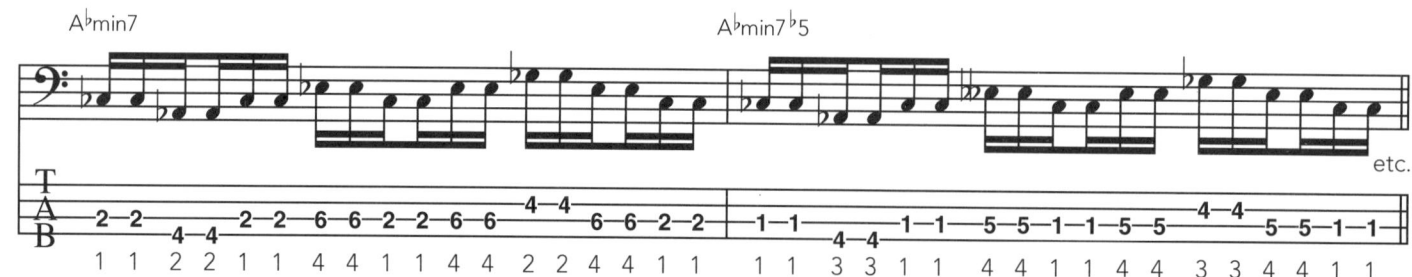

34 SECTION FOUR—The Workouts

Day Sixteen
Warm-Ups #1-4
Bassercise #16

This exercise is based on half-step *approach notes* to dominant 7 chord tones. Approach notes are notes one half step away from a chord tone, in this case, one half step below. The approach note is played just before the chord tone and then resolves upward to it. To help you better understand how approach notes work, the chord tones in Bassrobic 14A are circled. The other notes are approach notes.

As you sequence this one-measure pattern chromatically up and down the fingerboard, keep your hands relaxed and concentrate on making each note sound good.

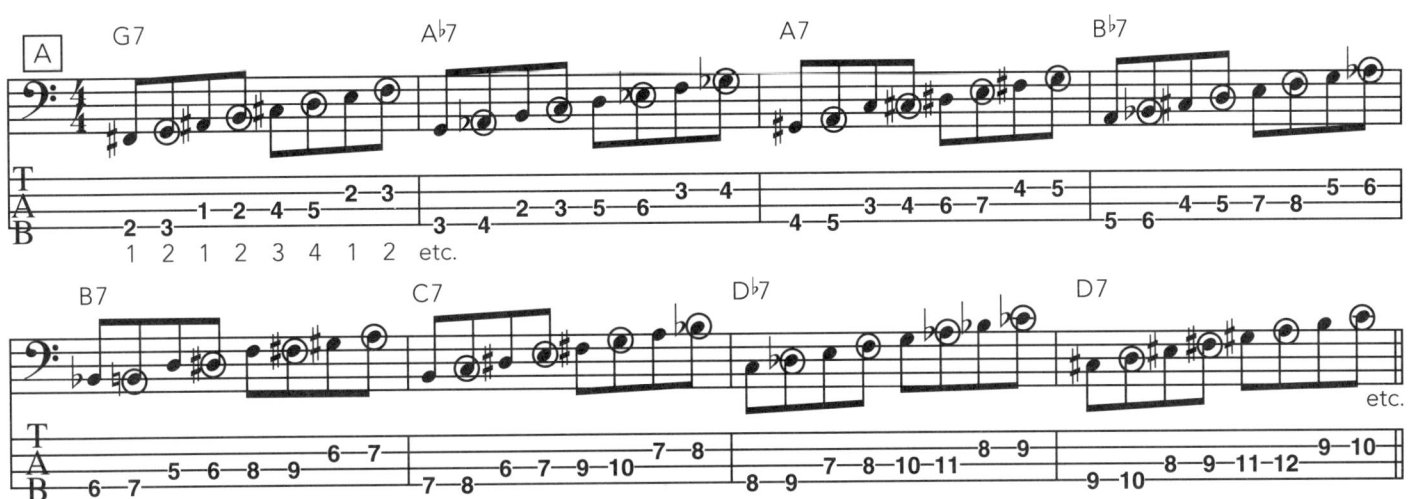

This is the same exercise starting on the 3rd string. As always, sequence it chromatically.

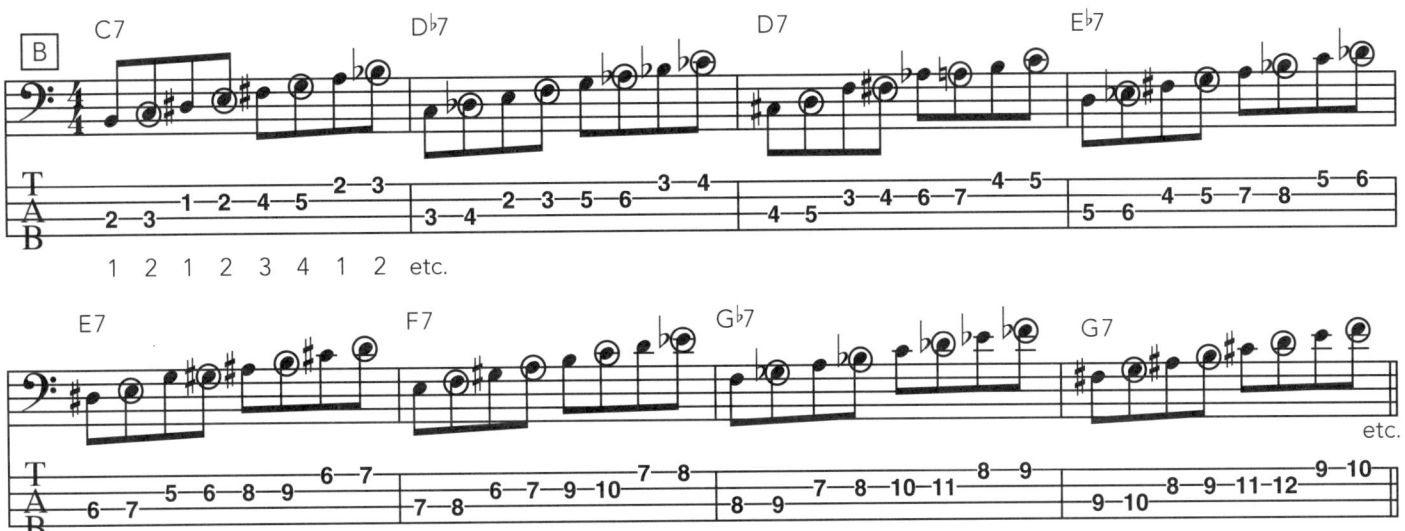

SECTION FOUR—The Workouts

Bassrobic #16

This is a workout for the right hand using half-step approach notes to dominant 7 chord tones. Be sure to alternate the 1st and 2nd fingers. Concentrate on making a good sound on each note. Play this exercise starting on the 4th and 3rd strings and sequence the one-measure pattern chromatically up and down the fingerboard.

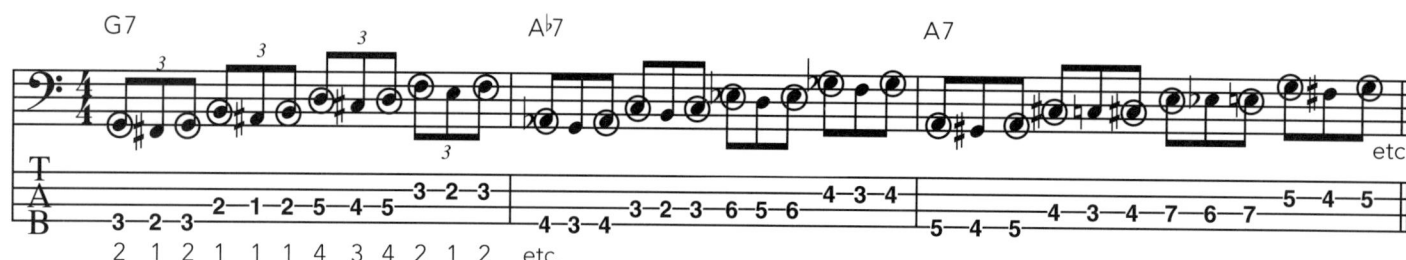

Day Seventeen
Warm-Ups #1–4
Bassercise #17

This exercise is a single-string workout. Sequence this one-measure pattern chromatically up and down the fingerboard and across all four strings. Concentrate on keeping your left hand relaxed.

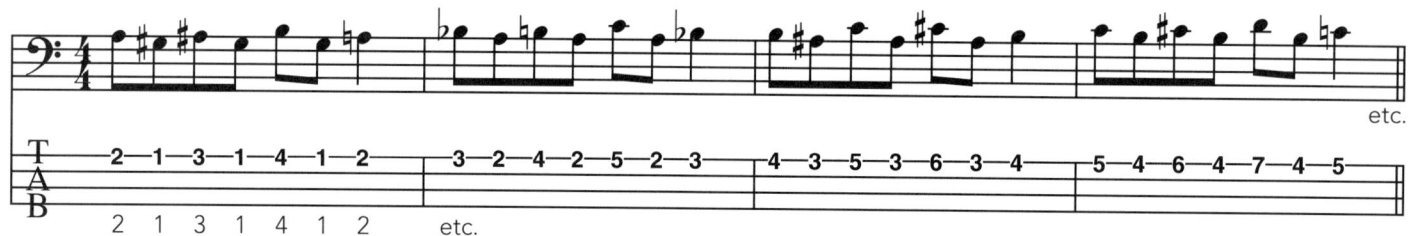

Bassrobic #17

Although this exercise is written on the 2nd string, practice it on all four strings. Sequence this four-measure pattern chromatically up and down the fingerboard. Concentrate on getting an even sound with your right hand when playing the sixteenth notes.

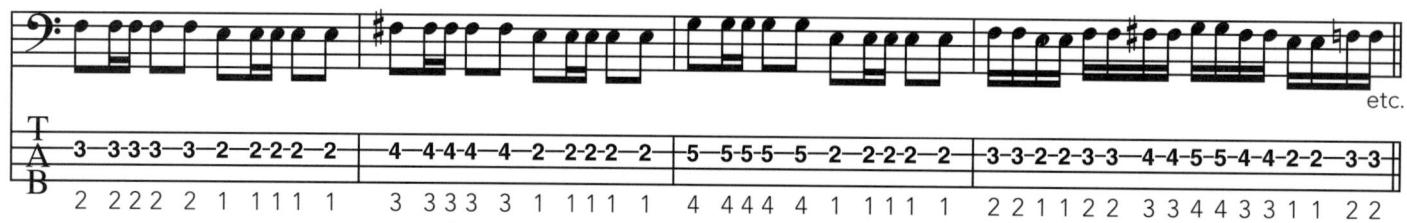

Day Eighteen
Warm-Ups #1–4
Bassercise #18

This exercise is another workout to help strengthen the muscles in your left hand. As always, sequence this one-measure pattern chromatically up and down the fingerboard. The exercise in written starting on the 3rd string but be sure to practice it on all four strings.

Bassrobic #18

The rapid-fire sixteenth notes in Bassrobic #18 should be played slowly at first. Then, accelerate the tempo gradually until you can play it accurately at breakneck speeds. If you have any doubt that sixteenth-note grooves are common in contemporary bass playing, listen to the playing of Jaco Pastorius and Rocco Prestia (Tower of Power). This will give you another good reason to keep practicing these exercises! Sequence this one-measure pattern chromatically up and down the fingerboard and on all four strings.

SECTION FOUR—The Workouts

Day Nineteen

Warm-Ups #1–4
Bassercise #19
Bassrobic #19

Today is one of your review days. Practice the exercises from days 12–15. Be sure to practice them across all four strings of the bass whenever possible. This is a good time for you to practice these exercises at even faster tempos.

Day Twenty

Warm-Ups #1–4
Bassercise #20
Bassrobic #20

Today is another review day. Practice the exercises from days 16–18. Be sure to practice them across all four strings of the bass whenever possible. This is a good time for you to practice these exercises at even faster tempos.

Rocco Prestia (born, 1951) is held in the highest esteem for his work in Tower of Power. His driving sixteenth-note bass lines have become classic in the bass world. His influence as a stylist and individual voice on the electric bass are unparalleled.

Day Twenty-One

Warm-Ups #1–4
Bassercise #21

The exercise is based on the interval of a 6th, which is the distance of either eight (minor 6th) or nine (major 6th) half steps. This requires that the left-hand fingers stretch across the strings. Play the exercise very slowly at first and concentrate on keeping the left hand as relaxed as possible to make the stretches easier. Sequence this four-measure pattern chromatically up and down the fingerboard.

Bassrobic #21

This exercise also uses 6ths. It is a little tricky, as the right hand must cross strings while playing triplets. Concentrate on keeping the right hand relaxed as it crosses the strings. Maintain an even tone. Sequence this eight-measure pattern chromatically up and down the fingerboard.

SECTION FOUR—The Workouts

Day Twenty-Two

Warm-Ups #1–4
Bassercise #22

Here is another exercise based on the interval of a 6th. It is very difficult. It demands crossing the strings between the 1st and 2nd fingers of the left hand, and also between the 2nd and 3rd, and 3rd and 4th fingers, all the while playing steady eighth notes. Start playing at a slow tempo. Take your time as you sequence the two-measure pattern chromatically up and down the fingerboard. Play this exercise starting on the 3rd string as well. Keep the left hand loose.

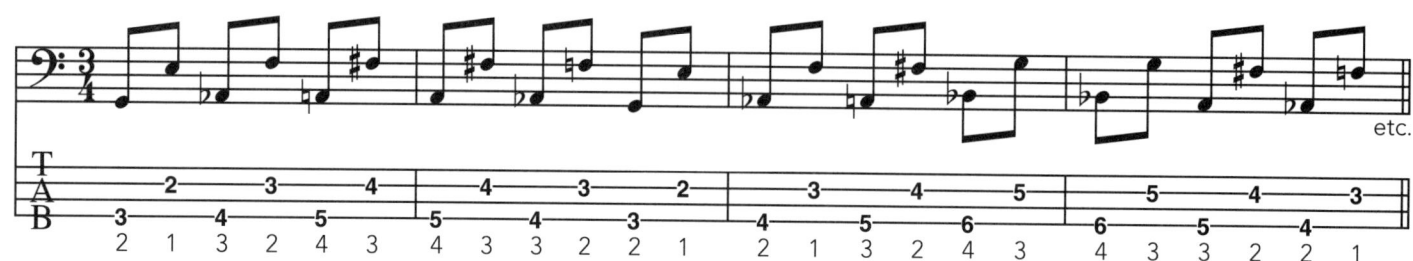

Bassrobic #22

This exercise is similar to Bassercise #22, but the right hand must cross strings while alternating fingers in triplets. Sequence this one-measure pattern chromatically up and down the fingerboard. Play starting on the 3rd string as well. Concentrate on maintaining an even tone.

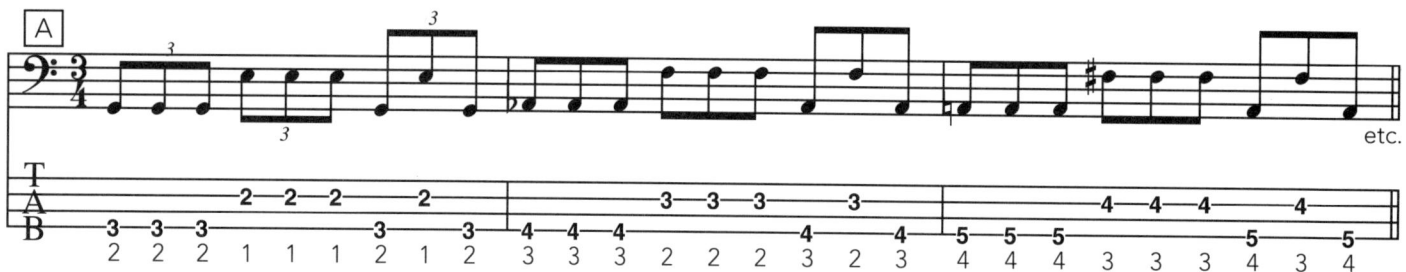

This exercise consists of 6ths in sixteenth notes. Sequence this one-measure pattern chromatically up and down the fingerboard. Also practice starting on the 3rd string.

SECTION FOUR—The Workouts

Day Twenty-Three

Warm-Ups #1–4
Bassercise #23

These exercises use *hammer-ons*. To play a hammer-on, pluck the first note of a pair with the right hand, and then hammer onto the second note with the left-hand finger forcefully enough to make it sound (without plucking with the right hand). The challenge here is to achieve the same volume on the hammered note as for the plucked note. Play slowly at first. Practice chromatically up and down the fingerboard and on all four strings.

H = Hammer-on

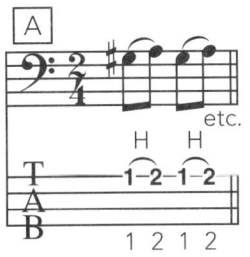
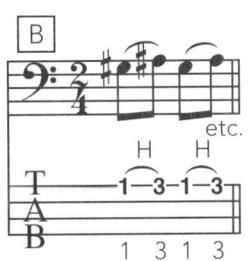
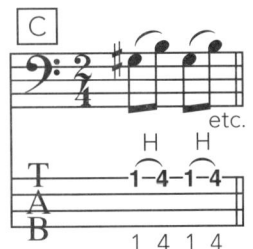
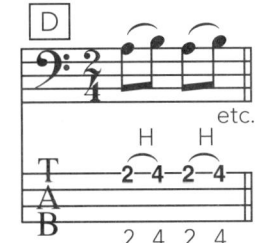
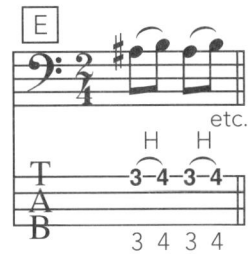

Bassrobic #23

These patterns use hammer-ons and sixteenth notes. Concentrate on making the plucked notes and hammer-ons sound even. Sequence these exercises chromatically up and down the fingerboard and on all four strings.

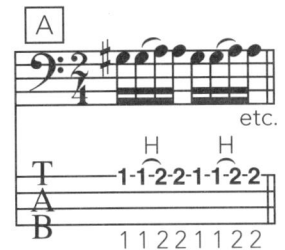
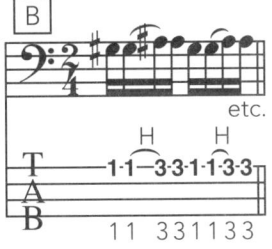
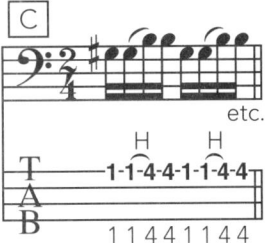
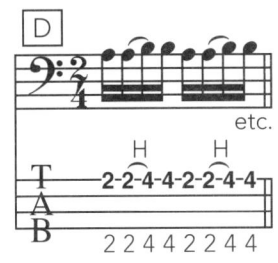
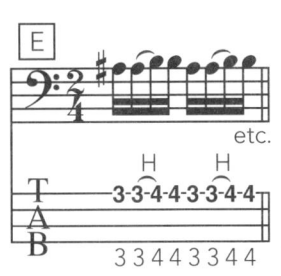

Day Twenty-Four

Warm-Ups #1–4
Bassercise #24

These exercises give the left hand a workout through different combinations of fingerings with triplets and sixteenth notes. Practice these patterns chromatically up and down the fingerboard and on all four strings.

SECTION FOUR—The Workouts

Bassrobic #24

These exercises will help you build strength, agility and stamina in both the right and left hands. Sequence each pattern chromatically up and down the fingerboard and across all four strings. Concentrate on getting a good sound on each note.

Day Twenty-Five

Warm-Ups #1–4
Bassercise #25

This exercise uses triplets, hammer-ons and *pull-offs*. Pull-offs are played by pulling a left-hand finger downward and away from the string to make a lower note sound without being plucked by the right hand. Strive to play the hammer-on and pull-off notes equal in volume, and to make them both as loud as the plucked notes. Practice slowly! If your hand gets tired, take a break, but see if you can eventually play this exercise chromatically up and down the fingerboard and on all four strings.

P = Pull-off

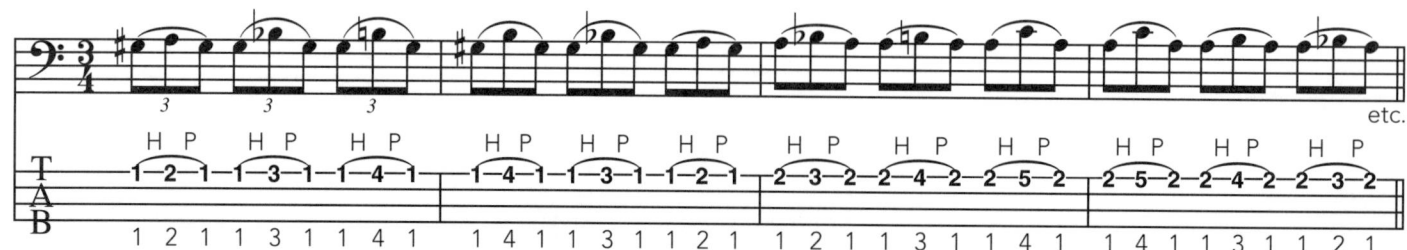

SECTION FOUR—The Workouts

Bassrobic #25

This exercise uses hammer-ons and pull-offs. The hammer-ons and pull-offs occur between adjacent fingers (1st–2nd, 2nd–3rd, 3rd–4th). This is a great workout for building strength. Sequence this exercise chromatically up and down the fingerboard and across all four strings.

Day Twenty-Six

Warm-Ups #1–4
Bassercise #26

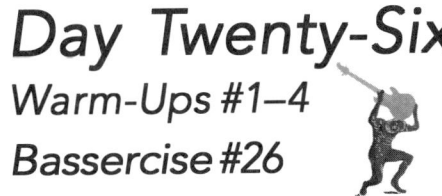

This is a great exercise for developing agility. The one-measure pattern has four permutations of a three-note group from the major scale, and is played on every step of the scale. Sequence this exercise chromatically up and down the fingerboard starting on the 4th and 3rd strings. The finger pattern must remain unchanged.

Bassrobic #26

This is a great exercise for building speed and agility, using only three different notes in a pattern. As always, sequence this three-measure pattern chromatically up and down the fingerboard. Practice starting on the 4th and 3rd strings. Have fun!

SECTION FOUR—The Workouts

Day Twenty-Seven

Warm-Ups #1–4
Bassercise #27

These exercises entail crossing strings and playing *octaves* (twelve half steps). Some players use the 1st and 3rd fingers to play octaves, while others use the 1st and 4th fingers. In these exercises, use the 1st and 3rd fingers on the first octave of each measure and the 2nd and 4th fingers on the second octave. Sequence the patterns in these exercises chromatically up and down the fingerboard.

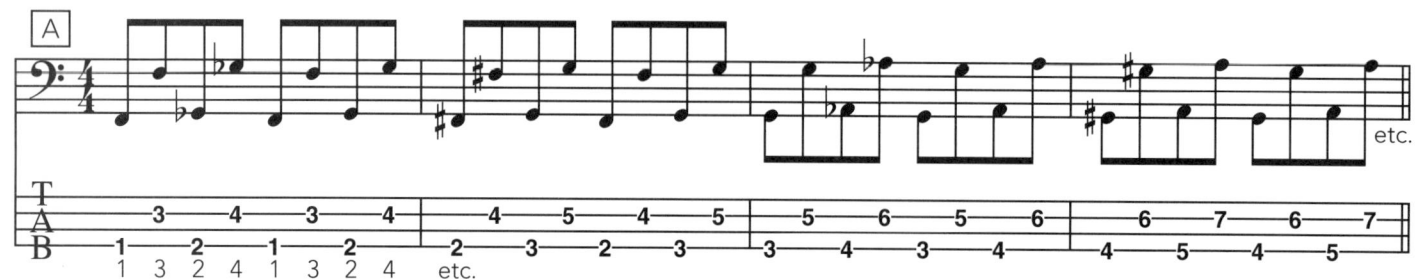

Bassrobic #27

These exercises also involve octaves, but in *double time* (playing each note twice, twice as fast). This exercise will get you on your way to playing some very funky sixteenth-note grooves. Sequence these patterns chromatically up and down the fingerboard.

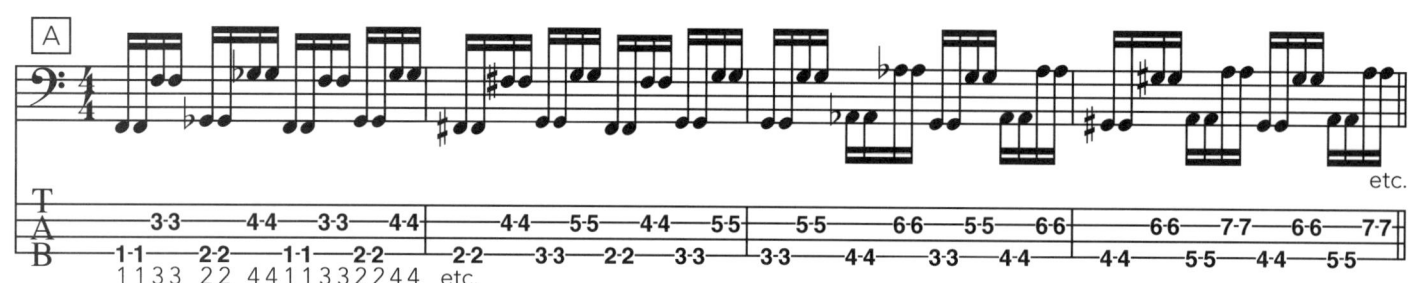

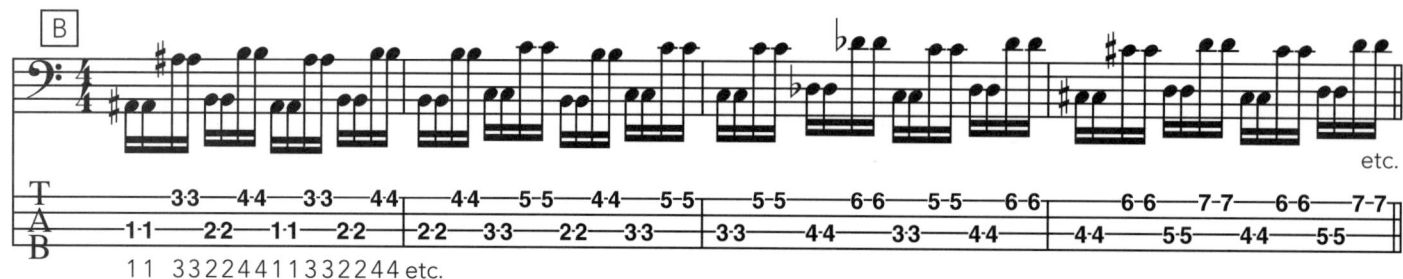

SECTION FOUR—The Workouts

Day Twenty-Eight
Warm-Ups #1–4
Bassercise #28

This exercise is based on a chromatic, one-measure pattern. Keep the left-hand fingers limber. Sequence this pattern chromatically up and down the fingerboard and across all four strings.

Bassrobic #28

This exercise has you playing major triads through the *cycle of 4ths* (the root of each harmony is a perfect 4th—five half steps—above the last). Concentrate on getting a good sound out of each note.

SECTION FOUR—The Workouts 45

Day Twenty-Nine

Warm-Ups #1–4
Bassercise #29

Sequence these one-measure patterns chromatically starting on the 2nd, 3rd and 4th strings. Concentrate on keeping the left hand relaxed.

Bassrobic #29

This exercise prepares you for those Jaco Pastorius and Rocco Prestia sixteenth-note grooves. Strive for an even tone with the 1st and 2nd fingers of the right hand. Play this exercise starting on the 3rd and 4th strings and sequence the two-measure pattern chromatically up and down the fingerboard.

Day Thirty

Warm-Ups #1–4
Bassercise #30

These exercises require the use of extended fingerings. Take your time as you stretch for each note. Sequence these patterns chromatically up and down the fingerboard. Practice exercises A and B and across all four strings. Practice exercises C and D starting on the 4th and 3rd strings.

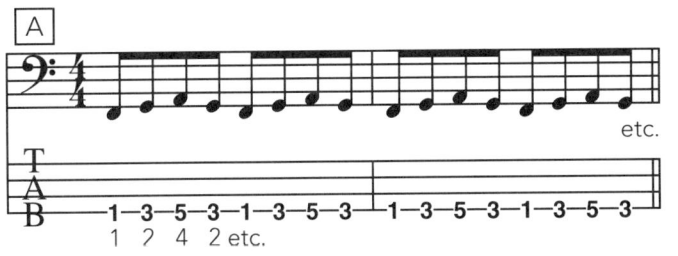

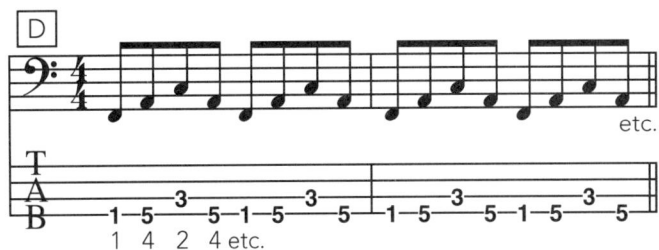

Bassrobic #30

These exercises will give you a great right- and left-hand workout with extended fingering and sixteenth notes. Sequence each exercise chromatically up and down the fingerboard. Practice exercises A and B on all four strings. Practice exercises C and D starting on the 4th and 3rd strings.

Congratulations! You have made it through the 30-day workout. Now, go back to the beginning and enjoy another 30 days of great practice. Remember, this part of your practice routine is only about technique. You have lots of other musical work to do. Get to work!

SECTION FOUR—The Workouts

IF YOU ENJOYED THIS BOOK, YOU'LL LOVE OUR SCHOOL
NATIONAL GUITAR WORKSHOP

Guitar
Bass
Voice
Drums
Keyboards

Rock
Blues
Classical
Alternative
Songwriting
Acoustic
Country
Fusion
Jazz
Funk

1-800-234-6479
NGW • BOX 222 • LAKESIDE, CT 06758
Call or write for a free brochure.
www.guitarworkshop.com